A Mother's Story

A Mother's Story

GLORIA VANDERBILT

ALFRED A. KNOPF   NEW YORK   1996

Grateful acknowledgment is made to the following for permission
to reprint previously published material:
The Dalton School: The poem "Sonnenkinder" by Carter Cooper (first
published in *Blue Flag,* the literary magazine of The Dalton School,
Vol. 35, No. 2, Spring 1982). Reprinted by permission of
The Dalton School.
The Journal of Allergy and Clinical Immunology: Excerpts from
"Psychological and Somatic Interrelationships in Allergy and
Pseudoallergy" by David J. Pearson (*The Journal of Allergy and
Clinical Immunology*, Vol. 81, No. 2, 1988, pp. 351–360). Reprinted by
permission of *The Journal of Allergy and Clinical Immunology.*

ISBN 0-679-45052-1

Manufactured in the United States of America

First Edition

Carter lives in the memory of his friends and in me, his mother, and in my son Anderson Cooper, to whom this book is dedicated for his strength, courage, and bravery and for the love he gives to me.

A Mother's Story

I

SOME OF us are born with a sense of loss. It is not acquired as we grow. It is already there from the beginning, and it pervades us throughout our lives. Loss, defined as deprivation, can be interpreted as being born into a world that does not include a nurturing mother and father. We are captured in an unbreakable glass bubble, undetected by others, and are forever seeking ways to break out, for if we can, surely we will find and touch that which we are missing. I hope you don't live in this invisible glass bubble, but if you do I am one of you. I know it well, and as the years passed, I sometimes recognized it in the eyes of strangers and sometimes in the eyes of those I loved, and when it was not there I rejoiced. Those without it were far ahead of me and always would be. From the beginning their base was mother and father — to turn to, rely on, always there to cocoon the inevitable blows that come to us. If sometimes I envied them, I told myself that perhaps I was the fortunate one. Perhaps without the unbreakable glass bubble the stab of pain is even deeper, because it is unexpected, unprepared for. Those of us who are born in the glass bubble are already prepared and never quite that surprised — each loss somehow echoes that first loss, the one we know so well. Something falls into place, so familiar it is almost a relief. Though we may be outsiders, maybe it's not so bad after all. Still, all my life, with each loss I have tried to break out of the unbreakable glass bubble. But instead of breaking out, I found myself breaking inward, each loss stripping me closer to a deeper layer of myself, yes, closer and closer, until I came to the final loss, the fatal loss that stripped me bare, the loss that had no echo, no memory of anything that had come before: the loss of my son Carter Cooper, a loss I thought I could not survive. But I did. The unbreakable glass didn't. And that's what I want to tell you about.

2

MY FATHER, Reginald Vanderbilt, died when I was fifteen months old, but as I was unaware of this, it wasn't until many years later that I lost him. You can't lose what you never had, or so I thought. It was only by chance, when a friend and I were talking about self-esteem and I mentioned my lack of it growing up and she said, "That's because you never had a father." It was a revelation to me, for *that* had never occurred to me. Not having a father had obliterated a whole part of my life, but I'd never missed it. It was as if she had taken a brush, dipped it in white paint, and suddenly swooped it across my heart, leaving half of it rattling around somewhere in that unbreakable glass bubble that held me. I kept looking at her in a totally new way. She had often spoken to me about her parents, about "Papa," the house she was born in, the house she still returns to, her mother there, although

5

her papa died when she was twenty. It had all been real to me, but real as a fairy tale is real. When she talked about Papa, I absorbed every detail but really hadn't a clue what she was talking about. Now I did. I understood her confidence. The pride she carried herself with had come from the gift of self-esteem Papa had given her, and some small part of me started forgiving myself for feeling unworthy, for that is what I felt, although what it was I felt unworthy about, or why, still eluded me.

3

I wish my mother, Gloria Morgan Vanderbilt, were living in New York today, somewhere very near, just around the corner, so I could go round and have a cup of tea with her, talk to her as I never had been able to when she was alive. She has been dead about thirty years, and when I think of her, which is often, my relationship with her keeps changing. I perceive her in ways I never had before, and as I do I come closer to her, and so, of course, to myself. The last time I spoke to her was on the phone hours after Carter was born. She and her twin sister, my Aunt Thelma, were to have come from California to be with us for the birth, and because I had two sons by a previous marriage, my husband, Wyatt Cooper, and I hoped for a girl — and my mother did too. But as the time approached she became gravely ill and was unable to make the trip. I knew she was dying and for a desperate moment was going to lie to her that our wish had been granted. I wanted so much to please her, to make her happy to know that there would be a Gloria after she died, a Gloria after I died, a Gloria named after her as I had been. But I didn't. I told her that she had a beautiful new grandson and that he was named Carter Vanderbilt Cooper. There was a pause, and then she said, "Why, Gloria, you're going to start a baseball team." I laughed with her, but what I really wanted to do was cry — cry for having disappointed her again, cry for not being able to break out of myself and tell her how I'd longed to be close to her. Yes, even in the years of my childhood when I'd been made to fear her, all I wanted was for her to love me, touch me, so that I could merge into her. And even now I wanted to tell her how sorry I was that I hadn't been born the boy she and my father had wished for — he already had a daughter by a previous marriage. But he had taken it "rather well," she had told me when I was seventeen, "when it turned out you were a girl."

Yes — she was unattainable, always out of reach — no sooner did she come into a room than she was gone, I never knew where. But with the years I have come to understand it was not her fault — she was too young to have a child. But then some women never should, and I suspect she was one of them.

8

They are narcissistic, too passively self-involved and unable to extend themselves. It never occurred to my nineteen-year-old mother or to my forty-four-year-old father that it was in any way singular, immediately after my February birth in New York, for them to take off for Europe, leaving Naney Morgan, my maternal grandmother, and Dodo, my Irish nurse, to take the newborn to Newport, mother and father not returning until August in time to supervise the annual fancy-dress ball given at my father's 240-acre estate, Sandy Point Farm. It is not surprising that these two women, maternal grandmother and devoted nurse, became the only real parents I came to know, love, adore, and feel safe with. They were the only real home I ever knew. Nor was it unpredictable when my father died unexpectedly a year later that my twenty-year-old mother, widowed, beautiful, rich, couldn't wait to shake free of Newport and move to Paris. Today, I understand her eagerness. Newport was Newport — and after all, it was 1925, and Paris was Paris, and it was all somewhere out there waiting to pursue — fun — life — that elusive *it* which will make our lives magical, brilliant, happy-ever-after. Of course I didn't understand any of that then — not until now, years later. Then, happy and safe though I was, bumbling around in my unbreakable glass bubble with my two devoted substitute parents — something was missing. It was an apparition that came and went. Sometimes it came up close, looking at me through the glass, smiling before disappearing. Would it ever return? And who was it? Mother — I was told. Oh . . . so that's who it was. That's whose attention I kept trying so frantically to get. Later, after we moved to Europe, sometimes I even desperately scribbled notes to my father — throwing them into the sea from one of the many ocean liners we seemed always to be on, or from fast-moving trains in dark tunnels, car windows as we sped towards Monte Carlo or through the green of an English spring. (Had he loved my mother? Had he loved me, that almost-infant blob of life he'd left without saying farewell to? And if so, why didn't he come back, and why had he left in the first place?) But as these specks of crumpled paper wadded into balls crashed angrily through the glass bubble, they disappeared without a trace — for my father was dead.

4

ON DECEMBER 7, 1977, Wyatt Cooper had the first of a series of massive heart attacks. He was in New York Hospital from then until he died on the operating table, January 5, 1978. He was fifty. At the time, Carter was twelve, Anderson ten, and they both attended the Dalton School.

Carter graduated from Princeton in 1987, while Anderson was completing his sophomore year at Yale. From college Carter went on to become a contributing editor at *Commentary,* and later an editor at *American Heritage* magazine. He was well on his way towards the future he looked forward to.

On July 22, 1988, in New York City, Carter Cooper took his own life. I was there when it happened, and I thank God it was me and not his father, who could not have survived. But I may be wrong about that — I thought I couldn't either, and I did. It was an aberration — a terrible accident — a misadventure — a mystery — then as it is now. Those of us who knew and loved Carter are still trying to find answers.

5

ALTHOUGH I was born to the branch of the Vanderbilts that built The Breakers in Newport, an infant knows only the presence, or lack of, food and warmth, light and darkness, the bliss of being held. These were the things my Naney Morgan and my nurse Dodo surrounded me with in the glass bubble. Had I been born into poverty or in a jungle, and been given the same love they gave me, my infant person would not have known if I was rich or poor. Later, as I became more aware, I came to know that I had not been born in a jungle, nor in poverty. I had been born into a very rich family who lived in a castle, and although it was never talked about I soon came to suspect that when it came right down to it, to my family, money was the bottom line. But to me it wasn't and never has been. I remember reading somewhere, "It's what you are inside that matters. You yourself are your only real capital." The money I later inherited through the efforts of my ancestors seemed suspect to me, perhaps because it was so sacred to Naney Morgan and the others in my family. Money — that powerful god was always floating up there somewhere, worshiped, bowed to, and courted. And when they did this, it changed them into persons I could not admire and did not trust. It was this that very early on gave me a fierce desire not to have to depend on others, to make my own mark. And, later, through my own talents, discipline, and hard work, I multiplied my inheritance many times over — and this is the money that is real to me, because it came to me through my own efforts.

People's attitudes towards money are always of interest, and I was fascinated by Carter's. While at Princeton he kept a notebook recording daily accounts of his expenditures down to the penny, as had a writer he so admired, F. Scott Fitzgerald. Carter was determined, and knew he was going to grow up and be an important part of our world. He dreamed of making the world a better place, and of plans for himself, too, for he wanted a family. Fair of face, golden and true, with the intelligence and the energy to pursue his dreams, Carter cared about everything. Sometimes as a small child he would become overly preoccupied with worry about what was happening, not only in the present but in those past worlds he loved to read about, and Daddy, trying to bring him back to the moment, would caution, "Carter — *enjoy, enjoy.*" Idealistic though he was, he was drawn to politics, and these meticulous lists were perhaps used as some sort of crossword puzzle, part of a map at the start of a long journey, exploring roads, turning points — for more than anything else he wanted to be in control of his life. No — Carter wasn't born in an unbreakable glass bubble. From the beginning, until Wyatt Cooper died twelve years later, Carter had a father, a father who like him wasn't born in a glass bubble, and it was through Carter's father that I gleaned an intimation of what it must have been like not to have been born in one. And I want to tell you about this, about what Carter and Anderson's father was like, so that you'll understand where he came from and why he was able to give me a sense of what it must have been like to have a family. And through this, although I could not break out of the glass bubble, there were times when I could bring them into it with me. And when I did, I knew I had a family too.

6

AFTER A bitter custody battle between my mother and my aunt Gertrude Whitney, in the 1930s, I had lived, since I was nine, along with the nurse I adored — Dodo — who had been with me since birth, on my aunt's estate at Old Westbury, Long Island. As long as Dodo was there, no matter where I was, it was home and everything would be all right. I had started going to Greenvale School and making lots of new friends, always knowing that when I got back to Aunt's at the end of the day, Dodo would be there. Then, without warning, on a New Year's Day, she was taken away from me and I was told I'd never see her again. But Naney Morgan wasn't taken away, and she sometimes visited Old Westbury. She lived in faraway New York City at the Hotel Fourteen. I'd call VOlunteer 5-6000 every night on the dot of seven, but that wasn't enough for me. I wanted more.

Being Chilean and volatile, *she* had no problems with glass bubbles, but it was hard to pin her down, as she tended to go off on gossipy tangents about European royalty, especially her dear friend the infanta Eulalia, in which I had no interest at all. As for Aunt and glass bubbles — let's put her at the top of the list — *she* didn't communicate about anything, and certainly never about nurses or mothers or custody cases. I longed to talk, ask her why my greatest fear had come to pass — why Dodo had been so suddenly sent away and why I'd never see her again. Aunt was powerful — surely she could bring her back! But Aunt would only smile and suggest "it might be better to talk to the lawyers about it." Once I tried, but they fidgeted uneasily, avoided looking at me, and when I asked one of them, "Will you be my father?" it was a *big, big* mistake. All he could do was blubber out words that made no sense, scurrying out of the room as quickly as possible. I sat there stung with mortification and shut myself up in the bathroom. But that's no criticism of Aunt — rich people brought up in that time and place were the exceptions if they *did* communicate with their children. After all, Mother hadn't, so why should Aunt? One of the things I learned very early on was that if you cry you go into the bathroom and shut the door. And when you come out you keep silent and pretend it never happened. I also learned that there were two things never talked about — death and money (not necessarily in that order). Funerals were gotten over as quickly as possible, money discussed only by grown-ups secretly amongst themselves and their lawyers. I remember going to Piping Rock Beach Club the day after some members of the club had been killed in an automobile accident, parents and children all dead. Eyes averted, the grown-ups didn't talk about it. No one did. They went to the funeral, of course, but that was different. You got through things without crying or showing emotion. The important thing was to keep everything moving smoothly along and not get too close, for that would never do.

7

WYATT COOPER was born on a farm in Quitman, Mississippi, in 1927, was graduated from high school in New Orleans, and attended the University of California in Berkeley, and UCLA, where he majored in theater arts. He became an actor on stage and in television, an editor, and a writer.

We met at a small dinner in a friend's house in New York. From the first moment we looked at each other, before we even said hello — there was a shock of recognition between us. We knew we would be not only important to each other but together and part of each other for a very long time. We were both in our mid-thirties and I had two sons by a previous marriage. He had never been married, and as we came to know each other, we both knew that we wanted the same things — a life, a family together. Maybe our child would be a girl. After all, there were five sisters in his family before he was born, and my mother had a twin sister — under these circumstances daughters might be in our future. I fervently hoped so.

The wide wedding band he designed was crafted by Buccellati. Inside, his words, engraved:

Gloria — Wyatt — together without fear — trusting in God — in ourselves — in each other — with hope — faith — and love

When he gave it to me he said, "Lots of happiness ahead for you, little one." And what he said that day did for many years come true.

8

THE HOUSE in which our children were born was on East Sixty-seventh Street in New York — a five-story graystone reminiscent of a house in Paris where I had lived as a child. Two stone lion sculptures we found in a New Jersey quarry were placed on either side of the stone columns of the entrance. Inside, we wanted to make the house look as if it had been there always and would be there forever, a house that had been in a family for generations — our family.

To be pregnant has been for me each time the supreme joy. It is my greatest achievement, and it is hard for me to understand women who sometimes complain about the discomfort and loss of self-image they experience when they are pregnant, because I never felt so centered, so beautiful, so loved, so important. I loved my body and my spirit as never before. Each day came as a miracle. There was not a moment when I didn't feel my best self. I was doing the greatest thing in the world without having to do anything — all I had to do was *be*.

Carter Vanderbilt Cooper was born on January 27, 1965, Anderson Hays Cooper on June 3, 1967. Anderson's first name was Wyatt's mother's maiden name, and Hays was from a Cooper cousin and, coincidentally, from my maternal grandfather, Harry Hays Morgan.

9

SOON AFTER Carter was born, his father and I took him to meet his Cooper relatives in Mississippi — most importantly, his father's *mother*. I had not met her before and was very scared, putting endless worry into imagining the moment, overly preoccupied with what to wear and how I was to avoid telling his family that I'd been raised a Catholic. After much silent pondering I put these two questions to Wyatt. It was decided that it might be wiser to tell them, *if* the subject came up, that I was a Unitarian. Although Wyatt had long since questioned the religion in which he had been raised (as I had mine), his family came from a long line of firm Southern Baptists who did not look favorably on Catholics, and I did want to make a good impression, so this little fib I hoped would be forgiven. But what to wear? How about a Chanel suit? These questions resolved, I didn't give them another thought.

Wyatt's parents had nine children. The first five, daughters — and then a boy, Wyatt. This first son had been heralded throughout the South. His oldest sister once said to him, "Why, there was never a child in the world as adored as you were! And it wasn't just us. Everybody did!" It has been said that everyone in the South is related, and I certainly felt that on that first trip with Carter, as we entered the house in Tuscaloosa of Cousin Frank Rose, president of the University of Alabama. Overwhelmed, I found myself tongue-tied and somehow threatened by the many unknown relatives and friends welcoming us with a warmth so unlike what I had grown up with. I felt more of an outsider than ever, believing that their life-long closeness to my husband put me way in the background, if present at all.

Wyatt came from a southern storytelling tradition whose writers are sometimes accused of exaggeration. On the contrary, as he himself has written, the alterations they make upon the actual are more often in the direction of simplifying the truth for the sake of credibility. When he introduced the name of Bobby Joyce Raspberry into conversation, for instance, or that of Aunt Della Belcher, or of a great-grandmother named Doll Flowers, or told stories about Cousin Emma Boykin, who painted angels on her ceiling and gave each one of them her own face, his northern friends' sympathetic smiles told him that they thought he was borrowing from southern fiction in a gallant attempt to make himself interesting.

So, apprehensive though I was, I had looked forward to meeting the family I had heard so much about — and now here they were. But there were so many, and I couldn't seem to grasp which name went with which face or who exactly was related to whom and through what branch of the family. No doubt I was more than a little jealous, too. Everywhere I looked there was a whole world of something I'd never had, and *they* had it. Family. *They* had known the man I loved from the beginning — they held *first* place. I was only the guest.

Southerners' hospitality is legendary, but at the time it seemed there was so much food to eat, one sugary meal just over and another about to start, and always more people to meet. I couldn't think of a thing to say and must have appeared a cold northerner. I was unable to show how much their welcoming joy and love towards Carter — and towards me, too — meant to me. Yes — there I was too shut up in my glass bubble to allow it to get through to me.

10

WYATT WAS sometimes asked if Carter and Anderson were aware of the part my family has played in American social history, as if there were some singular circumstance in being a Vanderbilt that required special handling in telling one's children about it, and he was reminded of Sarah Churchill's reply when asked what it was like to be the daughter of Sir Winston and Lady Churchill. "It was like having a father and a mother," she said.

The answer, of course, as Wyatt said, is that they do know, and it seems no more novel or particular to them than it would if the name were less well known. No more tact or discretion was required in relating Vanderbilt stories than when he talked about his own less glamorous ancestors. Carter was fascinated by architecture and the preserving of landmarks; his principal interest in Vanderbilt history had to do with houses. He liked The Breakers at Newport better than Marble House or the house at Hyde Park; he wondered why Bergdorf Goodman, instead of tearing down my grandmother's Victorian mansion that covered the block on Fifth Avenue between Fifty-seventh and Fifty-eighth streets, couldn't have left it standing and simply set up shop in it and in doing so, preserved it for posterity. He was curious about what sort of persons built the houses, particularly his favorite, Biltmore, at Asheville, North Carolina, and was fascinated by the fact that the estate had its own railroad and that the hundreds of acres of grounds were laid out by Frederick Law Olmsted, who designed Central Park. When he watched the *Masterpiece Theatre* series based on the life of John Churchill, the first duke of Marlborough, and his ambitious duchess, he followed it with avid interest. He loved all things military and was delighted to discover that the present duke of Marlborough was his relative through the marriage of Consuelo Vanderbilt and the ninth duke. Consuelo, later Madame Balsan, had written a book, *The Glitter and the Gold,* and in it are pictures of Consuelo at Blenheim, the enormous palace built for the Duke by Queen Anne and a grateful nation and named for his most celebrated battle, pictures of her in velvet and ermine as a canopy bearer to Queen Alexandra at the coronation of King Edward VII in

1902, and others of equal interest. We talked about the marriage itself, which was a most unhappy one, arranged out of Mrs. Vanderbilt's intense social ambition, and on the duke's part, out of his need for cash.

Both boys liked the idea that it was their great-great-great-grandfather William Henry Vanderbilt who brought to New York and had set up in Central Park the Egyptian obelisk called Cleopatra's Needle, around the base of which they often played. Because the personalities in family histories intrigued their father, he told them stories about the old Commodore, some favorable, some not so favorable. Carter loved the plan that the Commodore submitted to Abraham Lincoln (never put into effect) that he should personally load one of his ships with bales of cotton, set it afire, and ram the dreaded iron ship the *Merrimack*. When we watched another television series, on American history, Vanderbilts were discussed in connection with great American fortunes, robber barons, and lavish living, and we'd talk of it as of any other matter about which one need feel neither shame nor pride. The boys seemed to understand that any family, whatever its name, will include some persons of fine character, some of less, some who contribute and some who are useless, and we knew that the boys' sense of their own worth would not depend upon the fame of their forebears.

Yes — we talked about things, we were a family. Once on a morning after Alfred Lunt and Lynn Fontanne came for dinner, Miss Lynn spoke to me on the phone and said, in her slow, precise way, "Alfred tells me that he had a most interesting conversation with your young man, who I believe he said was seven. They talked about Tolstoy, and Alfred thinks the child might be some kind of genius. Now, you know geniuses have a reputation for being somewhat difficult?" When I told Wyatt this, he smiled and said, "He hasn't shown signs of being difficult, and he's not a genius. What he is, quite simply, is included." And he was. Carter and Anderson felt that they were participating because they *were* participating. And sometimes I was too. Sometimes they were there in the glass bubble with me. But I was still pounding to break out.

11

ONE NIGHT late, midnight or so (Carter was eleven), his father was working, typing at his desk down the hall from Carter's room. Suddenly Carter appeared in his pajamas, standing there, talking as if he were awake. But he wasn't. Several times before he had walked in his sleep, but this was the first time he was saying sentences that seemed to have no connection with this sudden visitation. As he spoke, Daddy quickly typed out Carter's words, and when he stopped, carried him back to his bed, sitting beside him until he was certain he was really asleep. Next day we showed Carter what he had said, but he had no recollection of walking down the hall or standing talking to his father or of being carried back to his bed, and was most amused by this sleepwalking/ talking event. I'm telling you about this because it connects somehow with what happened later. I don't know quite how, but I think it does, and you'll see why when I tell you about it. I'd give anything in the world to have that piece of paper with Carter's words on it. It's in a box somewhere along with my papers (I save everything) — boxes of papers spanning the years — reams of paper, notes for stories I want to write some-day, snips of dialogue heard on a street corner, telephone messages, every letter ever received, pages of childhood diaries — the list is endless. Or it could be in one of the many files of Wyatt's papers, which I have not yet gone through because I am unable to de-cide which university to donate them to. Or it may be that I postpone, can't let them go, because I miss Wyatt so much. I am haunted by the thought that if Carter's sleepwalking words could be found, they would give us clues. This all ties in with Carter's dread of taking naps in the middle of the day, because they always disoriented him. On that Friday afternoon of July 22nd he'd fallen asleep on the sofa of our library — the heat was unbearable, but he hadn't wanted the air conditioning on. I'd been with him, went out for a minute, and when I came back he was stretched out on the sofa, asleep. I went to wake him, but hesitated. He hadn't slept for several nights, he was exhausted — so I let him sleep. After Carter's death I tormented myself, and still do. Had I not hesitated, had I awakened him, it might not have happened.

31

12

ONCE, WHEN he was five or so, Carter, with his strange intuitions, asked his father suddenly and without preamble, "Did you like your father very much?" Wyatt was startled, but told the truth. "No," he said, "I didn't," and he told him why. Mostly it was that his father made him feel so bad about himself. He used to yell at him when he performed ineptly, as he invariably did, at rugged tasks. He remembered vividly an occasion when he was hardly tall enough to reach the handles of the plow he was trying to guide through the wet ground of a cane patch. The wet earth makes the plow go deep, and it is hard to control. Certainly his strength was not sufficient, and as the plow wobbled back and forth, his father stood at the end of the row yelling, "You'll never do it! You're no damn good!" Carter, in telling the story to me later, added an observation of his own: "And naturally, that made Daddy do it that much worse." Carter had got the point all right. It certainly did, and it is strange that Wyatt's father would not have noticed that result. He seems to have been a bully and a tyrant, and he had no idea of the effect he was having.

13

THERE ARE varying degrees of apprehension involved in the first meeting with the mother of the man one loves. As for mine, it was acute — not only fear that she wouldn't like or approve of me, but even if she did, would I be *worthy* of that approval? I'd been shown photographs of her, and she had often been described to me — her inner serenity, the strength of character, the blend of poise and feminine containment that she maintained throughout her life, and an acceptance of the wayward contradictions of living which was almost Oriental. While each of her children had something of their father's hysteria in his or her nature, their mother was like the calm in the middle of the storm. She brought one back to reality. Her voice was rarely raised, but her observing eye was full-visioned and unbiased, and her grasp of the main argument was quiet, clear, and complete. She had brains and character and concern (and, incidentally, a good head for business), and those were good anchors to hold on to. She was the strength of the family, the pillar around which it revolved. She was not without physical vanity and had always kept a treasured lavender ribbon from a box of candy she'd once won for being "the most modest girl" in half a dozen counties. She'd always been told that she was beautiful and rather came to expect it. Above all, she was completely and simply herself, always and all ways the same, without guile, pretense, or artifice. She was incapable of affectation, and other people's airs and graces made her laugh. She was discreet and understated, and — unlike the rest of the family — not likely to volunteer criticisms, flattery, or judgments. Asked for an opinion, she gave an honest one, considerately stated, devoid of exaggerations, and her view usually took in all the relevant possibilities. Impressive, isn't it? It certainly is, and of course I was pea green with envy. How different she sounded from my own mother — the mother I never really knew, the mother I was estranged from. This other mother I kept hearing about loomed before me like the Statue of Liberty, while my own remained like a beautifully posed still photograph taken from a movie, silently taking up most of the space inside my head and affecting everything I did in one way or another. The fear and anger I felt towards my own mother hadn't diminished as the years passed, and I listened enthralled as I heard about this other mother, so perfect in every way. I was jealous and confused, and when I did meet Wyatt's mother, I drew more and more into the glass bubble, and we had little to say to each other. It is still a sadness to me that she died before we ever really came to know each other.

14

Wednesday — Oddly unnerved and insecure most of the day. Then joyous times with the children. Daddy's mother, stepfather, and other relatives are arriving tomorrow. Hope all will go well. Once in Meridian visiting Daddy's family I called my Aunt Thelma in California for no reason except to hear her voice — just to know she existed, that *I* too had a relative.

Later — Well — they arrived. At lunch when we were all going in, Daddy pulled out my chair and said, "Mrs. Cooper" — it was so sweet of him to do that, he knew how much it would please me and make me feel *the* most important — but, as he did,

37

his mother moved to sit there — assuming he meant *her* and not me.

Thursday — Carter asked his grandmother "Why would a good God do it?" about some biblical horror and she said, "Well, God doesn't have to do things like that anymore." I wanted to (but didn't) answer — No, He only does things like Belsen, Auschwitz, Vietnam, and lynchings in the South. I expected Carter any minute to say, "Mommy doesn't believe in God," but Daddy changed the conversation quickly. Actually, I do believe in God, but it had become too complicated to go into my feelings about the Great Intelligence.

15

WYATT'S PATERNAL grandmother's family had originally come from Virginia, and they were poor relations of the Wyatts who were among the first families to settle in the Virginia Colony, with roots that went far back in English history. His grandmother had wanted to call Wyatt's father by her family name, but his grandfather did the naming and so he was named Emmett, and Emmett was thinking of this when he gave his own son the name Wyatt. Wyatt's father, Emmett Cooper, was the second son in a family of thirteen children. Emmett never spoke of his older brother with anything like affection, and he never spoke of his father in any way that suggested warm personal feelings, only smoldering resentment, enormous respect, regretful admiration, and a deep-seated (but desperately fought-against) sense of his own failure to measure up to his father's stature. But he always spoke with tenderness of his mother. Wyatt always said that it's from your mother that you first get a sense of your worth. The warm softness of her body, the protective support of her arms, the sustenance that comes from her continuous presence, the soft soothing sound of her voice, her response to your outcries, are the first awareness you have, and from these things come your first feelings of being wanted, valued, and treasured. Wyatt told me that his father got his sensitivity and his tenderness from his mother, but that he was never able to feel comfortable about or know quite what to do with either. As Wyatt described his mother — it could have been a description of the love Dodo had given me as a baby and later as a child. Yes, I too had had a mother — until I was nine, anyway. Two mothers, really, for I had Naney Morgan as well. So why hadn't that been enough? Why did the elusive Other have the power to fill me with fear and longing?

16

AFTER MOTHERS, fathers interested me the most, and Wyatt's father, Emmett Cooper, in particular. I was told he had instilled in Wyatt something of his passion for the land, his kinship with nature. Wyatt's earliest and most pleasant memories of him are connected with nature: standing close to him in the darkness of night when all was clear and silent and still, and gazing up, up, through countless miles, into the endless expanse of stars over them, while he pointed out the Little Dipper, the Big Dipper, and the mysterious North Star, which was always north, and because it was, you could never be lost, no matter where you were. Or at daybreak pausing with him in the front yard and peering with him at those first streaks of light across the sky that told you, if you knew how to read the signs, what kind of day was promised. Or moving with him in the soft, sweet haze of early morning through fields of dew-covered grass, and feeling all life beginning to stir around you. Or sitting beside him inside the door of the barn while he smoked and watched the rain falling outside.

Evidently, Emmett had more than a little madness in his makeup; he was possessed by a wild vision of life, and a seething discontent plagued him into prolonged and terrifying fits of rage. Yet certainly his children knew and took for granted that the major drive of his life was for his family and that all that was left of his hopes and expectations was tied up in them.

Wyatt said he was a strange man, complex and contradictory, and that when Wyatt thought of him now, when he pictured his face or when he started to describe him, the person he thought of was very different from the figure he thought he knew when Emmett was alive. He saw his father then as a towering figure of potency, threat, and menace, and lived in fear of and in resistance to all that he held his father to be. Long after his father died, Wyatt was given a photograph of him taken when he was seventeen. He looked at his father's boyhood face, and, incredibly, it was the same face he was to meet for the first time twenty-three years afterwards, sad and remote, anticipating rejection, with dark, wounded eyes turned inward toward remembered pain. The pose is tentative and unsure, and suddenly Wyatt remembered his fa-

42

ther's movements, which were at some moments unbearably uncertain. There was no hint of the gaiety and high spirits of which he was capable, or of the animal grace with which he sometimes carried himself, or of the charm and magnetism with which he could, in an expansive mood, completely captivate the unwary; there was no indication of his delight in narrative or the pleasure with which he held his audiences. In the picture there was only the apprehensive look, as if he might at any moment take flight, and the hooded, suffering eyes, and Wyatt said he wondered how in all those years with him he had failed to see it.

Actually, Wyatt said, there was no mystery, and he did not fail to see it. The truth was that it was only one step from the woeful eyes to the look of madness that he recalled. When the volcano of anger and frustration erupted inside Emmett Cooper, those same eyes burned with rage and destruction and he struck out widely and blindly, accusations, curses, ranting insanities pouring from him in a sustained explosion directed at his absent father, at Wyatt's mother, at his absent mother-in-law, or at the heavens, or at the absurdity of existence — an ongoing outburst that seemed somehow as madly logical as Lear on the heath shouting into the thunder. Wyatt said he now knew why his father was not physical in these outbursts — he never struck either his mother or the children. The punishment was only verbal, the cruel and compulsive lashing of a venomous tongue. And the punishment, Wyatt now understood, was directed at himself.

When Wyatt's father died of a heart attack, Wyatt was seventeen. It was too late for grief, he said; he'd felt grief for him in the past, when he was alive, grief for the awkward, accusing, wounded silences between them, grief for what had long since been lost or rejected or perhaps had never been, grief for a seventeen-year-old misunderstanding that was probably inevitable but which had injured both of them without either of them understanding that he had the power to diminish the other. It was only later that he would understand that his father had feared him as much as he had feared his father. This was also true of me and my mother. We had been estranged for many years, and when we did get to know each other a little towards the end of her life, she told me how frightened she had been of me as a baby, afraid to pick me up, hold me. And then as I grew up I was taught by everyone around me to fear her, and she in her passivity couldn't see beyond herself and I became an even greater object of fear to her than she had been to me. It was only after she died that I came to understand what had happened — too late, of course.

After hearing stories about Emmett Cooper, I'd

think about him a lot — about Wyatt and his father. And then I'd think about my father, Reginald Vanderbilt. And what did I know about him? Well, I knew a little about him from Dodo — his love of horses, the show horses he prized, and when I grew up I would have silver trophy cups to prove it. He had many friends and was well liked, gregarious, and . . . and — well, that was about it. His sister, the aunt I lived with, never mentioned him, but she did have his clay head sculpted by Jo Davidson on a windowsill in her bedroom. It was placed so that his eyes gazed out over the lawns stretching down the hill to distant meadows where cows grazed, and I in turn would gaze at him whenever I went into Aunt's room. As it was not Aunt's way to open up to me, I too kept silent, waiting for the subject of my father to come up. But it never did.

17

GRANDFATHERS CAME next. My grandfather Cornelius Vanderbilt II had died long before I was born, and I had seen my Grandpa Morgan only a few times before he died. One memory of him slowly walking with a silver ram's-headed cane as we made our way together along the boardwalk in Cannes one summer. "Hurry up, Grandpa, hurry up," I kept calling up to him — we were on our way for ice cream. My grandparents were separated by then and it was hard for me to connect my Naney Morgan's raging outpourings against him with the gentle teddy bear I kept urging to "hurry up." But there were many memories of Wyatt's grandfather, who was an overwhelming figure, an extraordinary personality, powerful and commanding even in old age, when Wyatt had known him. His name was William Preston Cooper and he was rich, influential, and well known in east Mississippi and

46

west Alabama. "Prominent Choctaw County Planter & Merchant Dies," the *Meridian Star* said in reporting his death. They were all in awe of him. Tall, proud of bearing, a full pepper-and-salt mustache, he was an unassailable presence, and when he appeared, his grandchildren stopped whatever they were doing — games were abruptly broken off, frivolity abandoned — and stood more or less at attention, all concentration focused on him. It was not that he demanded it — such people don't have to — he simply expected it, took it for granted, and it just happened, and not only with the family. One time when Wyatt and his father were in Kirkland's Store in Quitman, Grandpa entered. They stood unnoticed to one side while he made his progress through the store. Hats were removed and respectful greetings offered. "How are you, Uncle Pres?" "Mighty good to see you, Captain." And clerks rushed forward to serve him. He accepted the deference as his due, not even noticing that it was deference. His arrogance was so habitual that it seemed like good manners and came off as a gracious sort of condescension — he was never seen to behave toward anybody as an equal. He walked with a stiff coldness, and that day he moved behind a counter, as if he owned the store, to inspect some merchandise. Wyatt said, "I thought you weren't supposed to go behind the counter," and Emmett, without removing his eyes from the old man, said in a low, muffled voice, almost as if speaking to himself, "You're not." "But Grandpa did," Wyatt insisted. "He ought not to," Emmett said, and the bitterness and defeat in his voice, Wyatt said, he could still hear now, forty years later.

Grandpa dressed every day as if it were Sunday, and he was partial to white linen suits for winter as well as summer; with them he wore a spotless white Stetson hat. To judge a man, he used to say, you took a look at his hat and his shoes. Emmett, in turn, would get himself such a Stetson in a sudden burst of confidence, would look at it, turning it this way and that, and finally, with some pride, put it on. But he never really brought it off, and soon it would be put away to gather dust.

Grandpa owned a store, a grist mill, and twelve hundred acres of land, much of it virgin timber. He liked to ride about his land on his beloved gray mare, called Old Mag, and the tenants stopped their work and bowed respectfully as he passed by. This description of him, Wyatt said, rather misleadingly calls up an image of the sainted Robert E. Lee, whereas he actually bore a strong resemblance to Mark Twain, a somewhat different brand of fellow. And if some of his tenants knew very well that they sheltered under their roofs children bearing their names but fathered by

Grandpa (for he quite openly exercised the practice of *droit du seigneur*), it should banish forthwith any association with the austere General Lee.

18

THE QUALITY I most admired in Wyatt was his deep sense of responsibility. He felt an obligation about whatever specialness was his, and that obligation alternately thrilled and frightened him. He doubted his ability to fulfill it, and what he prayed for — and fervently — was that he should be dedicated enough, compassionate enough, and moral enough to meet the task ahead of him. He was aware of his weaknesses; he knew that he was sometimes selfish, conceited, greedy for admiration, ambitious for himself, and scornful of others. He knew that he was often silly and vain, that his thinking could be fuzzy and unclear, his knowledge superficial, and his motives mixed. It was pretty hard for him to accept these frailties as right and natural in a messiah — they did not square with his passion to banish all injustice, all suffering, all pain and distress, to heal all wounds, to lead the way into a full, rich, and joyful world in which all men lived together in peace and brotherhood. He submitted himself to his own rueful inquisition, and found himself wanting. He asked himself, as he had been taught to do in church, "Would Christ do what I'm doing? Would he feel in his heart what I feel in my heart?" — and too often, the only possible answer was that he would not.

As for me, his parenting to Carter and Anderson was something I had never seen before, nor could have imagined, and I, too, called him "Daddy."

19

Sunday — The beauty of this place with the children. Stan [my eldest son] a delight. I feel so secure when he's here. Started large oil of him late today. Head has odd composition — monumental. I want to get *into* it. Close. Merge with him. Receive the image *whole*. Later, Carter and Anderson ask me to tell them stories about when I was "little." It gives me great joy to invent things that never happened. Stories about me and my mother — the way I wish it had been. Telling them makes it true to me — almost.

Thursday — A day of clear crystal. The sound of the children calling to each other across the lawn. Anderson in a raspberry shirt — berry brown and freckled, blue blue of eyes. Playing in the pool — I whooshing through the water trying to catch him — a fat minnow. Carter brings me Queen Anne's lace — like white sparkler fireworks for a July 4th. He kisses me fervently.

20

I THINK of Carter at five leaving home for the first time without any of us to go to Disney World with his friend Carter Burden, looking big and determined and small and forlorn all at the same time. I think of Carter at four, lying in the intensive-care room after heart surgery with tubes in his nose, side, and arms. When a nurse approached him, he would lift his fingers, the only part of his body he could move, and say, "Wait a minute, Nurse." Startled, she would ask, "What is it, Carter?" and he would answer, "Tell me what you're going to do and I can help you." I think of Carter and his father — how they recognized themselves in each other from the very beginning. They thought alike and often read each other's thoughts, communicating with glances and half-smiles without the necessity of words. I think of Carter at about three walking along the street with his father when a man approached using a cane. Just as he was even with them Carter asked, "Why is that man walking with a cane?" His father waited until the man moved out of earshot and said, "It's all right to ask that, but we don't ask it when the man can hear it, do we?" Carter said "No" and, to make sure he understood, his father asked, "Why not?" and Carter replied, "Because it might hurt his feelings." O.K. That point made, they moved on. At the next corner, as they waited to cross the street, a little old lady, playing, as some little old ladies do, the part of little old lady, looked at him and asked with a sweetness she'd learned from the movies, "Is that a little boy or a little girl?" Dumb. He looked nothing at all like a girl. His hair was cut like a boy's, and besides, you don't call children little, not if you have manners, so his father replied with a coldness in his voice, "*He* is a big *boy.*" Carter recognized immediately that his father was putting her in her place. He knew she was old enough to know the lesson he had just learned, so he spoke up, enunciating clearly and distinctly so that his purpose was unmistakable. "Daddy," he said, "is that lady a midget?"

21

There are some people whom one is always happy to see, and for me, Carter was one of those. He was the first preppy I ever knew! The first well-dressed, dapper, and stylish teenager! I remember when he began working out, and I used to say, "Carter, you hard-bod hulk! You're only one step shy of Schwarzenegger!" and how he'd start grinning so widely that he looked like the Cheshire cat. And then he'd trot off to class at Princeton with that great mixture of pride and grace which to Carter was perfectly natural. We'd joke around about our flip-flop-opposite backgrounds, and Carter would mention old days at our alma mater, Dalton, and we'd both be dissolved in giggles instantaneously.

You know, Carter always spoke of his "mom Glo"

and Anderson with such affection and sweetness I just wish you could have heard him. He was awed by his little brother's African adventure and by his mother's success. In fact, I really think Carter was buoyed by the antics of us who were lucky enough to have been in his orbit and in his circle of friends.

I just want to say that after I moved to Los Angeles I would think of Carter, and those faraway thoughts would be of purity (which he had in abundance), of innocence (which was so integral to his charm and appeal), and of the glory days (of which he had so many and helped all of us to have as well). It is exactly these feelings I have when I remember Carter.

22

CARTER WAS a precocious child and soon found out that he was, and it was not an unmixed blessing for him, for sometimes unpleasant behavior is identified with the precocious child. But Carter handled it well, though he used to say of his friends with some puzzlement, "Bill doesn't know about Julius Caesar," or "He tried to mix Roman soldiers in with Crusaders!" Once we were going through the Metropolitan Museum and Carter was having a marvelous time pointing out things to Anderson: "That's from Egypt and they were about five hundred years before the Romans, and this is . . ." We noticed a lady following us about and she asked us, "Is this some kind of scientific experiment or something?"

But he really learned that he was unusual from taxi drivers. We would be returning from a movie (at five, he sat several times through the Russian *War and*

Peace) or other cultural experiences, and he would be bubbling over with excitement and chattering away — he had the diction and vocabulary of a Philadelphia lawyer. "I think Shakespeare was right," he might say of something in *Henry V,* for instance, and the driver would turn around and ask, "How old is that kid?" That didn't have to happen too many times before he realized that he could make them turn around, and since it's only one step from the thought to the deed, he would begin conversations in taxis that we knew were for the driver's benefit. Such a child realizes, too, that while he likes the praise, he also is a bit of a fraud. Carter instinctively knew this, and his sense of humor always pulled him back from going too far.

23

DADDY BELIEVED that roots in the past are a precious thing, and that it was not a matter of having *splendid* roots, with illustrious and distinguished forebears decorating the pages of history. The important thing about roots, really, is not how enviable they are, but that they are there at all. The real difference, he believed, is in feeling related. I was fascinated by this, because although I too had a family, I not only felt disconnected from them, I had never felt rooted to them in the first place; I was there under false pretenses, a changeling.

24

Saturday — After the movie a midnight swim. Daddy, Stan, Carter, and delicious fat minnow, Anderson. Heaven.

Monday — Anderson stretched out on the porch swing watching Sam, his beloved snake, curling around his hand, marveling that this wild creature actually belongs to him, the wonder in his voice as he says, "Sam, is dis all a dream?"

Wednesday — Carter and Anderson such perfect Beings it sometimes frightens me. "Oh, you make me so happy, Mummy," Carter says. His face as he runs towards me holding Queen Anne's lace behind his back to surprise me. His face, a flower — sunlit, flooded with a beauty that blinds me. I wish the summer and living here would never end. I hate the thought of New York and going back.

25

It was soon after Anderson's birth that the Cooper family came to New York to meet the new member. They arrived early that day and had already gathered in our living room. I hastened down and when I entered, Wyatt's mother stood up and started to hold out her arms to me — but I pulled back. She did too. The moment when she and I could have burst out of the glass bubbles keeping us apart was gone. A second chance never came.

26

Daddy had the first heart attack in 1975. It was called "a warning." His father had died of a heart attack at fifty, the youngest of his five sisters at thirty-eight. But this "warning" at the time had seemed unreal — more like a mild flu attack — and although he had gone to the hospital because of it, he kept minimizing it and was soon released.

Then, two years later, Daddy, Carter, and I went one evening to the theater to see *Your Arms Too Short to Box with God.* It was filled with the gospel singing we all loved and we had such a good time, returning home in high spirits. But the next morning he woke very early, even before Carter and Anderson were up, saying to me, "I'd better go to the hospital." On the way there, holding his hand, I kept urging the taxi driver to go faster, faster. But we were not in an ambulance and the driver was angry that I kept at him to break the speed limit. Minutes after we arrived, Daddy suddenly said he felt better, wanted to go home, and that it had really been unnecessary to have gone there in the first place. But the hospital wouldn't release him, and an hour later he was rushed to intensive care. I sat in a waiting room, eyes closed tightly, clutching on to the hand of a woman I didn't know whose husband was also in intensive care. I was knotted into a hard ball, burrowing deeper and deeper into the center of the glass bubble. I could not see the woman whose hand was also clutching mine — couldn't open my eyes to see her face, couldn't speak — but we were kept alive, tied with cords of steel, one to the other, as we sat there waiting, and I'll never forget her.

27

ONE DAY when Carter was three years old he asked his father, "When I get to be as old as you are now, will you be very old and getting ready to die?"

His father said that something turned over in his stomach. His eyes burned, and he felt a constriction in his throat. Carter had asked an elemental question. It deserved as honest and as simple an answer as he could give, so he said, "Yes, I will be, if I am alive in my eighties," and he told him what he hoped and believed to be the truth, that if he lived that long he would have known much of the joys and rewards of living. He would have seen Carter and his brother Anderson embarked well into their lives, and could expect to let go with some feeling that the more important part of him would live on in them and in *their* children. Carter could accept that, and after some thoughtful shaking of his head, he returned to his play.

He had begun trying to understand the fact of death some time earlier. After seeing the movie *Ben Hur,* he asked one day, "All that was two thousand years ago?" His father answered, "Yes." "And all the people who were alive then are dead now?" Again, "Yes." "And lots of people have been born since then and then got old and died?" "Yes." "And someday everybody alive now will be dead and there will be other people living here?" "Yes." There was no other answer to give. He had summed up the whole story very well. He thought it over for a few moments and he rendered a judgment. "It's a strange way of doing it," he said.

His father thought, Well, he's not the first one in history to whom that idea has occurred, but he came to a conclusion, accepted it, and was able to get on with his life in the light of that knowledge. It might not be exactly as Wyatt would have arranged it if he had invented mankind, but there it is, the central fact of our lives. Sooner or later we learn to live with it. It may be our tragedy, or it may be precisely that truth which gives our lives the meaning, the significance, and the perspective that they have. Wyatt believed that the accommodation we make with our knowledge of the transient nature of time may be the single heroic element in our lives.

28

I have often thought about the day that Carter and I would be best friends, and I have often imagined being an uncle to his children, and he to mine. That day will never come, but we must all take heart, for Carter is out of pain, and he is with my father now.

Carter was an honorable person, and however pained we feel now, we must feel joy for that, and we must carry on our lives, for we are not alone. All that has been, still is, and I will forever live with Carter by my side.

He will always be, as my father once described, "that same brave little soldier he was one day when he was three and I looked out my window and saw him on the way to the park with his mother and his baby brother. Carter was dressed in full Roman armor with a red plume bobbing from his helmet, and his cardboard sword was thrust fearlessly forward as if defying the world, every ounce of his plump little frame leaning into the future, eager and pushing for adventure, while his other hand held tightly on to the safety of his mother's skirt."

Carter's soul is golden and true. I knew him, I learned from him, and I loved him for twenty-one years, and for that I will be ever thankful.

29

LATER, WHEN I was permitted to see Daddy — he was stretched out, his eyes closed, as though dead, surrounded by machines with their chilling staccato beeping, each machine connected to another tube, pounding out indecipherable codes — I took his hand and said, "I love you." He opened his eyes and looked straight at me. "I know you do," he said. It was a blessing — the greatest thing he had ever said to me.

There had been times in the sixteen years we had been together, times when we were close, times when I couldn't break out of the glass bubble when we hadn't been, times when I thought he didn't know how much I loved him. But I did. And when he said "I know you do" — I knew that he understood and loved me as no one else ever had.

30

ALL DURING that December Daddy kept having one attack after another, going in and out of intensive care, losing weight. Each time he came out he'd be moved to a different room. "This is a terrible thing to do to you and the boys," he said. It was the first intimation I had that he thought he was going to die. I was jolted, and shot out at him — "You are *not* going to die." "I'm not?" he said incredulously. "No, you're *not.*" And I believed it.

31

Friday — A strange wind today, like a mistral. Very unnerving. Working on "Memory" collage. Then in evening came a calm. After dinner drove with Daddy and children to find the "Secret Lane." Ran out of gas. Then walked on the beach — the four of us. The children with flashlights. Walking by the sea — everything falls into place.

32

THE HOSPITAL suspended their usual visiting hours, allowing Carter and Anderson to visit their father when he wasn't in intensive care any time, day or night. Christmas was approaching and we were making plans for that day, gathering presents and planning to take a recorder so we would have our conversation of Christmas 1977 on tape. We had planned, long before his attack, to be moving soon to a new apartment. I'd take swatches of wallpaper and fabrics to the hospital for Daddy to see and we'd go over them together. We disagreed on one — he liked this one for the sofa, I liked that. No, definitely that one, I said. Afterwards, I tormented myself over my opinionated choice, kept at myself for not having agreed right away on the one he'd liked, agonizing that he'd died thinking the sofa would be covered in the other. Every time I'd see it in our living room after he was dead I'd think of this, for it *had,* of course, been covered in the fabric he'd chosen, not the other.

33

HE CALLED one morning very early and asked if I'd come over and read to him — right away. I rushed over to the intensive care unit he'd been moved to during the night and, sitting beside him, started to read the Faulkner he loved. "Don't read so fast," he said. I am a fast reader, and that day read even faster than usual, because if I did it would ground him to life. But when he said that, I tried to read more slowly, and then he said, "Something's happening — I don't know what it is — a feeling of doom. Something terrible's about to happen." I ran for the doctors and they asked me to go out while they surrounded him. As I left, one doctor, a woman small as a child, had the strength of Samson as she pounded her fists on his chest trying to revive him. And she did.

34

CHRISTMAS EVE we gathered Daddy's presents and the tape recorder and put them in the hall ready to take to him Christmas morning. But at dawn of Christmas Day he had another attack, more massive than any that had come before. He had been removed to another intensive care unit. Every time I would go in he did not recognize me. He was struggling for breath, in and out, laboriously assisted by the hundreds of tubes and bottles surrounding him. Others in similar desperate condition were placed row on row around the huge room. His body was fighting the machines and I kept talking to him, talking to him, but there was no response, no sign that he even heard me. Our annual family Christmas photograph for that year had been taken before Thanksgiving, and it had gone with him from one intensive care unit and hospital room to another. But now it wasn't there. I still didn't believe he was going to die.

35

HE STAYED there from Christmas Day through New Year's until the late afternoon of January 5th, when the doctors decided to operate. I followed him to the elevator on his way to the operating room. He was surrounded by nurses tending the tubes attached to him. There was so much equipment in him he was unrecognizable — what they were carrying was a body taken down from a crucifixion. When I went back to wait in a room where friends had gathered, a nurse called Angel whom I knew well, as she had been the night nurse on his floor, was passing by. Every night as she was leaving her shift, I'd say to her, "See you tomorrow," and she'd echo back, "See you tomorrow." But this time she didn't. "Be brave," she said.

36

MUCH LATER, as his sisters and my friends sat with me waiting in the dark midnight hospital, it was quiet, so quiet, silent, no sounds at all — until down the empty hall footsteps running, running, and suddenly the room filled with people telling me he was dead.

37

As I left the hospital going down in the elevator I was possessed — screaming inside the glass bubble, Everybody I love leaves, everybody I love leaves — the father I never knew, the mother I'd never be able to reach, the nurse I loved, the grandmother I loved. It was after midnight when I got home. Carter and Anderson were asleep. I went in to wake them and tell them Daddy was dead.

38

Tuesday — A kind of wild joy springs out of me as Carter surprises me with a lavender flower. Joy in my work, contented with Daddy. Everyday things like shopping at the A&P. We go at night — it's quiet — a certain fun about it. Long swim with children in pool. No work today but tomorrow hope to finish "Memory" collage. Less sense of anxiety that I'll die before I get some of it said. Expiated. Later more storytelling about "when you were little, Mommy."

Thursday — A strange day again, like a mistral. Nerves on edge. Drive to city in heavy rain and thunder. Mood changes when I arrived. Brought three oils in to the framers. Secure with Carter, Anderson, and Daddy. Content. More than most have in a lifetime.

39

"IF ONLY I could bargain with God for ten more years," Daddy said in the hospital, and then told me he wanted a pine coffin and, if my family allowed it, to be buried in the family plot at the Moravian Cemetery on Staten Island — "so the boys can visit my grave." If not, he would have been buried in Quitman, his birthplace; he did not want to be buried in Meridian, where his family had later moved.

His service was at the Unitarian church. The wake before had been private, with only family members present. The pine coffin closed — opened only once while we stood silent, Daddy's sister looking down saying, "He looks just like Papa." The coffin was closed. I was so knotted up in the glass bubble I wasn't even able to kiss him goodbye.

40

WHEN CARTER and Pearson, the girl he loved, had broken up, months before that July day, he had told me about it but didn't want to talk about it. At the time, I tried as intuitively as I could to sense his feelings. She and I had become friends, but since it had happened I hadn't heard from her. I respected his wishes and didn't want to intrude until he was ready to confide in me. Outwardly, he presented his usual self — confident, in control of his life. He liked his job at *American Heritage,* had many friends. Soon I was hoping he would get involved elsewhere and that he wasn't grieving over the breakup. He didn't seem to be, but there was no way of really knowing. He kept it all very much to himself.

I kept telling myself he was at the age of breaking away, making his own life — still, I constantly asked myself whether I should intrude more aggressively into his life. Back and forth I went, trying to reassure myself that I had found the right balance, knowing that had I been Daddy I wouldn't even be asking myself these questions, for they wouldn't exist. Then a few months later I went to New Orleans on business and when I returned told Carter that I'd sent Pearson a postcard, as she and I had often spoken of that city. He was furious. He walked out of the room, saying, "How about a little support here, Mom?" I followed him out into the hall, overcome with pain at my insensitivity, but the door to the elevator was already closing. When he'd said that, "How about a little support here, Mom?" it had never crossed my mind that I wasn't supporting him in every way possible. I kept going over and over what he'd said, trying to reach him on the phone, but it wasn't until days later that he returned my calls, and when he did he clearly didn't want to talk about her or what had happened between us.

I wished it had been me who had died instead of his father. Carter would not have shut him out. That communication they had, always had, would be there for him. I felt that then, and I feel it now.

41

What can I say to you? I can't stop thinking about you and Anderson. I can't stop thinking about Carter, and now I know it's true, that the things that happen in life can break a person in two. If it's like this for me, I can hardly bear to imagine what it must be like for you. Everything is haunted now. I keep looking around my room, lying on the bed where he lay beside me making me feel safe and strong. I keep going through the presents he gave me, the delicate antique boxes, the books, the jewelry. I keep going through those two years of my life, the two happiest years I've ever had, remembering all the things he gave me. A few weeks ago someone said to me about Carter: "He saw the beauty in you and committed to it." No one else has ever done this and it changed me. Carter showed me what it was to love and he loved what it was to be transformed by that emotion. It was as though I had been born again. And Carter did that for so many others. He saw the beauty when everyone else was blind, he could find it with his un- erring eye, and once he had found it, he made it pre- cious forever. Because Carter could never take things lightly, he could never take things for granted. He was incapable of dishonesty, of cruelty, or of a base or low action — of all the things that are sometimes crudely associated with strength. And yet seeing how strong Carter could be for those he loved, I have never once thought he was weak. The most I ever thought was that he was fragile, that he was too pure and beautiful for this earth, that he was formed out of some material so fine you could only touch it with awe.

When I think back on how much Carter gave me, it frightens me. I worry he had nothing left for him- self. And when I think back, I see so many times when I was selfish without even knowing it, so many times I let him down, so many times when I should have fought through his pride to be there for him. I walk down the street talking to him, I wake up in the middle of the night talking to him, saying, "How can I make you see how loved you are, please, please come back to me, give me one more chance to hold you." I know that everyone who loved him must be going through something like this and that it is the wrong way to think. And so I try to remember all the times I saw him happy, when I shut my eyes I see his face alive with light and joy.

Gloria, I always used to say to Carter, "How did you get to be so good? How did you get to be as good as you are? You should write a book called How I Got to Be So Good." I used to say it playfully, though I knew the answer. That kind of goodness doesn't just happen. You and Wyatt and Anderson helped to make him the good, tender, beautiful creature he was. Before I even met you, I said to him, "Your mother must be a wonderful woman for you to have turned out the way you did," and he said, "She is a great lady." He loved you so much. He was so proud of you, so eager to say, Look, this incredible person is my mother. He worried about you too — he was such a worrier, as we know. He used to say, "I want her to be happy, how can I help her to be happy and strong?"

So when I wonder what I can say to you, I can say he loved you more than anything. I can say that I will love you and be grateful to you forever for giving him life, for bringing him into this world. I can say that he will be there beside us like an angel when we are sad and suffering, but that in a way he will be even closer

86

to us when we are happy and laughing. Carter's expressive face was made for happiness. He had the greatest laugh: full-bodied, strong, rich with the joy of living. I know he is with us, urging us toward the time when we will be able to laugh again so that he can laugh with us.

The service was so moving. It was truly a thanksgiving for his life and that's what we will never forget, all he gave us and all we have to be thankful for.

42

WE HAD a Lincoln Continental in the garage, and earlier in the week of July 22nd Carter had called to ask if he could use it. He had a date on July 23rd, Saturday, with a charming girl named Beth, to drive her out to Brighton Beach, a place he often went with friends. He loved to sit on a boardwalk bench at twilight looking out to sea and later dine at one of the many Russian restaurants in the area. Beth has her own business, a gym, and she had at one time been my trainer. We had become friends and I was glad to hear she and Carter were getting together. He sounded excited about his Saturday night date and was looking forward. More than anything I wanted him to be happy, and this just might be the very thing coming along at the right moment, at the right time.

43

ON THE morning of July 22 Carter arrived unexpectedly. He now had his own apartment several blocks
from his office. It was Friday around eleven a.m. and
the hottest day of the year. "I'm moving back home,
Mom," he said, back into his old room on the top floor
where he had lived during his days at Dalton and until
he went to Princeton. How great, I said, but why not
take Anderson's room, as he was in Washington that
summer and later would be at Yale for his senior year.
The two rooms were next to each other, and when we
moved in the boys had had much argument about
which should have the larger room. Anderson finally
had won. The room had a fireplace and spacious terraces around the top of the building. Carter was
pleased about having Anderson's room and he went
over to the door leading from my bedroom to the terrace. The door was closed and he looked out longingly

across the river — "I can't wait to go to Southampton," he said. Our family house had been rented for the summer and I said we'd go there the day after Labor Day, as soon as the tenants were out. Then he came over and sat beside me on the foot of the bed. He put his arms around me and said, "Oh, Mom, I love you so much." I love you too, I said, and we both laughed because I had rollers in my hair and they'd gotten squashed against his head as he hugged me. Can you stay for lunch, I asked him, or do you have to go back to the office? "No, I'll be here." I'll make spaghetti, I said, and we'll have lunch together and talk. I had a meeting at twelve at home which would only take half an hour and looked forward to lunch and the afternoon with him, eager to know what had brought him to the decision to move back home. While I got myself together for the meeting, he went into the kitchen, where Nora, my assistant, who had known Carter since birth, was fixing lunch. Just then, Anderson called from Washington and I told him the good news and he said it was fine with him for Carter to take his room. I was almost ready when Nora came in to tell me the people had arrived for the meeting. I told her with joy that Carter was going to be moving back home. "Is he all right?" she said. "What do you mean, 'all right'?" I was almost annoyed with her. What could not be "all right" about his wanting to move back home? But I didn't pursue the matter. The people were waiting, and I was anxious to get the meeting over with so I could get back to Carter.

44

SONNENKINDER

I sit, by the river's dry bank
as the wind drives over
the yellowed land.
Here,
there is no sun, for the summer-children are departed.
taking with them
all the earth's pleasures,
their laughter,
their gestures
their charm
once shone with such brilliance,
their voices
in tones of golden delight,
once,
hung

like ornamental wreaths
about
    the marble columns.
Streaked with light,
their faces
    turned towards the East
    with hope
they sang their battle-cry:
    "live for the moment, youth is all"
    and the cry
drifting out over the water,
    held those who watched
    for a moment
in a perfect trance,
        but
with the faintest rustling of the breeze
    the spell was lost.
And now,
    I, looking down,
        see only
the tumbled-over carcasses
        of once-precious moments,
the dry husks of friends
        who now offer no relief.
The wind,
    tearing through the ruins
chirps,

its sound
joining
the parched cry of the cricket
and the shadows on the wall
(do you see the shadows on the wall?)
 are phantoms of the summer-children,
haunting me
with visions of what
once
  danced with life
   amid the ruins.

— Carter Cooper

45

THE MEETING over, I found Carter upstairs lying on Anderson's bed. There were two sliding glass doors covering the wall which looked out over the terraces and the East River, and in front of the river a walkway leading into the park. He had opened the glass doors and the heat in the room was overpowering. Don't you want me to turn on the air conditioning? I said, sitting down beside him. "No," he said, "it's fine the way it is." How about some lunch? I asked him. "That would be nice," he said. I told him I'd go down and arrange to have trays in the library. Years ago I'd discovered a recipe for spaghetti sauce that I'd make batches of and freeze, and this had become Carter's favorite meal. Soon it was ready and I went upstairs to him. He was lying on the bed as I'd left him, looking out through the doors towards the river. We went downstairs to the library and as we had lunch he told me he hadn't slept for several nights, and then he asked for more spaghetti. After you finish it, I said, why don't you stretch out on the sofa and let me turn the air conditioning on? "No, leave it as it is," he said, and after a while he stretched out on the sofa, asking me to cover him with a quilt and for a pitcher of water, he was so thirsty. Directly behind the sofa was a large window with a view of the river. He drew the quilt around him and stared out. I sat beside him — he looked at me and said, "Mom, am I blinking?" I was surprised, reassuring him that while he was asking me he had blinked several times. Carter, are you taking anything? "No," he said. Carter had never done drugs, although many of his peers had, and we had often discussed this. He was very health conscious, worked out at the gym, abhorred smokers, never drank anything more than an occasional glass of wine at a party. Drugs had no place in his past, present, or future — and, indeed, the autopsy performed after his death showed there were no drugs in his system. Once, after having a tooth pulled, requiring anesthesia, he told me how he hated the anesthetic because it had made him unconscious. He didn't want to miss a moment, a second, of life.

It never occurred to me that day to ask him if he was taking any doctor-prescribed medication. He'd had allergies and asthma since he was a child, and I knew he had chosen to go to a new doctor, but he had been reticent about it and I hadn't pressed. He seemed to be in charge of his life, and again I thought it part of growing up, of wanting to make his own decisions. Later, I discovered what the doctor had prescribed — a new respiratory inhaler. Soon after Carter's death I spent many hours with J. John Mann, M.D. — in 1988 at Payne Whitney in New York, later at the University of Pittsburgh's Western Psychiatric Institute and Clinic in Pittsburgh, and in 1995 at Columbia Presbyterian Medical Center in New York — talking to him, going over each moment, each detail leading up to Carter's death, trying to find answers to what had happened. Over and over, he kept coming back to the respiratory inhaler. Perhaps it would explain why Carter had requested the quilt and pulled it around him even though the day was so hot, why he was so hungry, so thirsty — would explain why Carter thought he wasn't blinking, why his eyes were glazed when later he came into my room before he ran up the stairs. This respiratory drug is described in the *Physicians' Desk Reference* as potentially causing central nervous system stimulation, and similar drugs in nasal sprays or drops have been reported to cause psychotic states. An article in *The Journal of Allergy and Clinical Immunology* (1988, volume 81, number 2) attributed "agitation, insomnia, terrifying nightmares and acute paradoxic, depressive states" to medications for asthma such as theophylline. Was his asthma worse and requiring the use of more medication? This drug was potentially both friend and foe.

Was the asthma a threat to his mind? To quote once again from *The Journal of Allergy and Clinical Immunology:* "Classic descriptions of the mental effects of hypoxia are to be found in the works of Haldane et al. and have since been amply confirmed. Marginal acute hypoxia produces subtle degrees of impairment of consciousness with poor judgment, diminished alertness, reduced attention span, difficulty in performing intellectual tasks, in judging time, and with memory, particularly in the area of new learning. Emotional symptoms can include emotional lability, irritability, or depression. Anxiety may be a notable feature of increasing hypoxia. There may be more obvious mental slowing, irrational fixed ideas, and uncontrollable outbursts. Without reason [the patient] may begin to laugh, sing, burst into tears, or become dangerously violent."

The article concludes, "The several mechanisms by which allergic diseases can lead to psychologic changes have generally been poorly acknowledged. We need to be more aware of the frequency of higher mental function impairment in moderate to severe asthma and of the nervous system side effects of many of the drugs that we prescribe. It appears very likely that misinterpretation of the significance of observations of such changes can be the origin of erroneous conclusions."

It is my belief that the new respiratory inhaler was the key to the demon that took Carter's life. That July 22nd, when I asked him if he "was taking anything," he knew I didn't mean any doctor-prescribed medication, which we both would have trusted, so when he said no, I knew that he wasn't taking any so-called recreational drug. Yes, he was relieved when I told him he had blinked, and we laughed about it. But I was puzzled. Would you like to call Dr. Young? I said. This was a cognitive therapist recommended by a friend, whom I had only recently heard Carter had started seeing. Later I found out that he had canceled an appointment earlier that week with Dr. Young, telling him he no longer needed to see him. No, he had no interest in calling Dr. Young. How about my reading to you? I said. We often did this together and it was one of my greatest pleasures. "That would be nice," he said, and after some discussion we settled on a short story in *The New Yorker* by Michael Cunningham —"White Angel." In the story, while his parents are having a party a young man runs and crashes through closed plate-glass doors that face a garden and he is killed. That's terrible, I said, when I finished reading. "It's a good story," Carter said, and it was. We discussed it for a while and then I asked him if he'd like me to read anything else. "No — I'll rest a bit." How about my getting a movie we can watch tonight? *"Road Warrior,"* he said. We've seen that so many times, how about Bertolucci's *1900,* just out on video? "Yes, I've been wanting to see that," he said, and I went into my room to get the number of the video rental to call. Then I went back into the library and asked him again if he wanted me to turn on the air conditioning. But he didn't, and I left him to rest, going back into my room, leaving the door open. It was unbearable, the heat. I'll be close by, I said — let me know if you need anything, I'm right here.

46

THURSDAY, THE night before Carter died, he'd made a call around midnight, a telephone call to Pearson, the girl he loved, the girl he'd broken up with. He wanted to see her — right away. It was late, it was raining, she needed to wash her hair, she wanted to look pretty for him, so they talked for a while — and then made a date to see each other for dinner on Monday, July 25th. It was four days away. The next night, July 22nd, Friday, she called my house at eight o'clock. Carter had been on her mind all day — she couldn't stop thinking about him and had been trying to reach him all day at the office, but he wasn't there and his number at home didn't answer. Nora, who answered our phone, told her what had happened. Stunned — "Is he all right?" she said.

47

FROM TIME to time that Friday afternoon, I had gone back and forth to see if Carter was all right. Every time I passed the open door going into the library he was there, still asleep, stretched out on the sofa. I was grateful I had decided not to wake him, that he was getting sleep at last after those white nights. At about seven I was in my room taking off a pair of earrings when suddenly the door opened and Carter came in. Dazed, he came towards me, saying over and over, "What's going on? What's going on?" There was nothing going on — the room was quiet, we were alone, there was no radio, there was no sound. Nothing's going on, Carter, no one's here except us, I'm here, Nora's here, we're all here, nothing's going on, the Bertolucci video's here, nothing's going on. I was standing close to him, speaking very softly, he was in a daze, and I kept talking, talking, softly, softly, trying to center him, bring him back to himself. He clearly didn't know me, or where he was, or who he was — disoriented like someone woken unexpectedly from a deep sleep, his eyes glazed. "No, no," he said, shaking his head, pulling away. I tried to hold him, but he had suddenly become determined — running like an athlete, fast, really fast, with purpose, energy, as if he knew where he was going, knew the destination. I ran after him, trying to pull him into the library — Carter, come here, I have to talk to you! I was panicked, almost screaming, trying to hold him, but he was running so fast, and although I had sneakers on he got way ahead of me as he raced through the halls, on up the stairs. When I got there, Anderson's room was empty. The glass doors were open exactly as they had been left that morning. There was a low stone wall surrounding the terrace, and Carter was sitting on top of it, about twelve feet away from where I stood, his right foot placed on top of the wall, the other on the terrace floor. What are you doing, Carter? I shouted, starting towards him. He put his right arm out, straight out rigidly in front of him, there was something military about it, extremely forceful, the palm of his hand held firmly out to warn me off. No, no, he said, don't come near. Don't do this to me, don't do this to Anderson, don't do this to Daddy, I was screaming, reaching out, straining towards him. Will I ever feel again? he said, and I screamed Yes, you will, I know what pain is and I can help you, Dr. Young can help you, and I started down on my knees, my hands begging out to him, and I was going to say, I'm your mother, but I didn't, because he shouted No no no to me, don't do that — and I quickly obeyed — got off my knees — stood there reaching out to him. Do you want me to get Dr. Young on the phone? I shouted. Do you know his number? he said. No, I said, and he got up from the wall, standing straight, staring past me, past the river, the distant bridge, staring ahead as if he didn't see them. He stood with a terrible rigid tenseness and strain, struggling, battling inside himself. Then he said the number loudly and very clearly — then he shouted out Fuck you, and I started towards him, but he had sat back again in the same position on the wall, only this time he was looking down at the walkway fourteen stories below, mesmerized, swaying back and forth. I stood there afraid to move, afraid it would send him down — shouting Carter, Carter. Then suddenly a helicopter passed above us, high up in the fading summer light — he looked directly up as if it were a signal, then turned and reached his hand out yearningly to me, and I moved towards him, my hand reaching for his, but as I did he moved, deftly as an athlete, over the wall, holding on to the edge as if it were a practice bar in a gym. He firmly and confidently held on to the ledge, hanging down over the fourteen-story building — suspended there. Carter, come back, I shouted, and for a moment I thought he was going to. But he didn't — he let go.

48

As soon as Carter started racing out of my room, on through the halls, up the stairs, I knew something terrible was happening, and when I saw him sitting on the terrace wall I could feel my spirit going up outside my body, at the same time remaining exactly where I was — but another figure that was also me was far up, high in the sky, looking down at the distant building we were on, the park to the right, the skyline beyond, and the scene happening below with two small people on a terrace, one standing between glass doors, the other sitting on a wall. From far away, standing suspended high up in the sky, I saw the whole scene as it progressed, right through from beginning to end. Later, in the days to come as I lay in bed, I would see it over and over again, but this time it was projected on a huge screen in front of me, unfolding in sequence, and when it came to the end it would run in reverse, the way a film does when it's being re-wound, and then start over again from the beginning. I am told this surreal removing of oneself, this looking down on what's happening, is a quite common experience during the witnessing of accidents, as is seeing a loved person who is dead in a crowd or from behind, hastening around a corner. This happened to me often after Carter died, and still does. The room I work in is on street level, and once when through the window I saw a young man pass resembling Carter so absolutely — I had to control myself from running out onto the street after him.

49

Monday — Read Daddy's script. Really good. Very proud of him. Slept late. The day breezy, almost cold. The children merry as larks. Carter says he'll never marry and wants to live with us forever. He wants to marry me. Declined going to the market with me because "it tires me, Mommy," then runs out naked into the hall to hug me and kiss me to make up for not going with me.

50

I RAN down the stairs to the kitchen. "It couldn't be," Nora said. Yes, yes, I kept saying. But she wouldn't believe me and said, "Come, let's go and find him." Together we ran up and I stood while she went looking over the wall, but she saw nothing and started running around the vast terraces looking for him. She was right, of course, *it hadn't happened.* But when she came back Carter wasn't with her. "I'll go down to the street," she said, and I went on down with her into my room and stood on the spot Carter and I had stood minutes ago. Something was in my hand — one of the earrings I'd been taking off when he first came into the room; apparently, I'd held on to it, but was only now aware of this. It had been in my hand as I ran after him up the stairs, onto the terrace, as I'd stood there shouting to him, reaching out to him — holding on to it as if it were a magnet that would pull him off the wall, back to me. Nora came in and said . . . police. Yes, yes, I urged, we must call them, do that, they are the authorities —*they* will be the ones to tell us *it hadn't happened*. I too started calling — Dr. Young, certain that he too, even a higher authority than the police, he would tell me *it hadn't happened*. But all I got was his voice coming from an answering machine, with no referral number to call, so I left a message. I had never met him and later when I did he told me that when he picked up his messages, Carter's name was cut off and he had sat up all night going through the names of his patients — dismissing Carter immediately as being the last person to consider. When he finally heard, he still couldn't believe it. I kept going through my address book, calling people, friends I loved, at random — certain that the next one was going to be the one telling me *it had not happened*. One man, a lifelong friend, just said, "Did he leave a note?" It was like a line of dialogue from a detective in an old movie — and the insensitivity of it may be fascinating to me now, but at the time it took my breath away.

51

SUDDENLY THERE were sirens, and the room was full of people. Dr. Tuchman, our family physician, was standing in front of me. *He* would be the final one to know. I looked close into his face, saw it so clearly, as I said, *Tell me it's not true?* I looked in his eyes and knew then that *it was true,* and I sat down on a bench in the hall and my mouth opened and a sound came — people were all around me, paramedics, one taking blood pressure, police were there, and the sirens, but the sound filling the rooms, filling the sky above, was not sirens — it came from an animal — on and on it went — but the sound was coming from me, and as it came — on and on — I split in two and the glass bubble cracked into a million pieces and was no more.

52

As a child and until I was about thirty, I often had episodes of crying, sobbing, but they finally ceased. I couldn't cry anymore, there were no more tears left. When Wyatt died I sobbed, but no tears came. Then, unexpectedly, I'd hear music, or see a scene in a movie, and tears would well up in my eyes. But I couldn't really cry. Now I could. I went to bed and cried — most of the time, in fact — going over and over in detail what had happened, again and again, over and over again, with each person I saw, each loving friend, each friend of Carter's who came to give love and support. I wanted to go over it again and again. The aura of reserve I had armored myself with all those years no longer existed. The glass bubble had burst. I was free.

53

I KEPT going over it, moment by moment, from the time he came into the room to the time it happened. I still go over it, now and every day of my life, agonizing over what I could have done to prevent it. Pretended to faint — he might have recognized me and come out of himself to help me. How stupid to have asked him for Dr. Young's number, I should have had the wit to tell him Dr. Young was already on the phone, come in to speak to him. I could have told him a car was downstairs — right now — waiting to take us to Southampton, where that morning when he first came into my room he had so longingly wanted to go. And I kept thinking how when I'd first seen him sitting there, my impulse was to risk the distance, rush across the terrace, and, with all my strength, try to pull him off the wall, but I'd discarded it instantly, as seeing me running towards him might have sent him over before I got to him. But maybe I *should* have done that. Then — had I been calm and spoken softly as I had before, before he started racing out the door, racing upstairs, spoken in the softly lulling sound I had used when he had first come into the room dazed instead of shouting to him when I saw him sitting on the wall — Carter, what are you doing? Had I done that — perhaps I could have saved him . . . But it happened so fast, my brain cutting in and out as if I were on an out-of-control roller coaster, trying to stop it.

I knew that if Carter had intended to take his own life, he never would have done it in our home, in front of me. Something had clicked him into something else, and the only thing that stopped me from clicking into it with him and following him over the wall was Anderson.

54

THERE WERE times I'd close my eyes and a blue light was there in the center of the darkness. It glowed like a jewel brilliantly lit from within — far away at first, then, slowly, closer and closer — becoming brighter and brighter. When that happened, I felt it to be Carter's spirit. When I opened my eyes it would be gone. Then I'd close them again to recapture it, but it would no longer be there — only darkness. Then — later — I'd try again and he'd be there.

55

MY BED had become a raft on which I lay far out to sea, and one by one, or in threes or fours, there would come a life support, a friend, climbing onto the raft to be with me. I stayed there sobbing and sobbing for days, without eating, without combing my hair or brushing my teeth, without changing my nightgown or showering, until the day of the wake — and they understood. I didn't sleep but took no sedatives or medication. I didn't want to — what I wanted was to talk and talk, go over it again and again, and that kept me alive in some strange way I still don't understand.

56

AFTER THE funeral, after Carter's burial in a pine coffin at the Moravian Cemetery on Staten Island next to his father, friends gathered at our house. Carter's friends, whose loving support had been with me constantly, were again by my side — I had only to look into their eyes to see Carter, and in mine they saw him, and in this we gave strength and courage each to the other. The door never closed as friends streamed through. There were moments I'd rush forward, certain that one of them bore a message from Carter — that he was late, delayed somewhere, and would be arriving any minute — but the message was not forthcoming. Still, as the day progressed, I persisted, going in and out of this wild hope, knowing that it would not come to pass but secretly believing it would. Soon Anderson and I would be alone, soon the rooms would be empty, the day ended. Soon Anderson would be returning to Yale to begin his senior year. A close friend, the last to leave, lingered at the door saying goodbye. His last words to me were "Now comes the hard part." And it was.

The losses in my life over the years had been many, each loss stripping me down to another layer, bringing me closer to the center of myself. But the loss of Carter had not stripped off another layer — it had exploded the core of what I had known myself to be, and a new self would have to be born if I were to survive.

57

I STARTED writing letters to Carter.

Monday — *Afternoon* — Carter — I don't know how to start this letter. It's a letter to you but it's really a letter to myself. I believe there is a logic in the world that comes from a Great Intelligence and that there is a reason therefore for all things and that we have our place on earth and have been born and placed here and there is logic and reason behind it. Carter, I'll never be the same. The pain I knew as a child I always thought of as my test and I imagined that nothing could ever hurt me in that way again. There was always a center hard as a diamond that no one could reach or take away from me. It was my final secret. But that is gone now and I am below sea level, centered there, balanced in pain that will never leave me. Walking on the beach I used to center down, always feeling grounded, because I had come to that great leveler — the sea. But I am now in another place, a place I didn't know existed, for now I know there is another level, a rock-bottom level from which there is no retreat, no surcease, and this is where I am. I am at the end of my life now and all I want is to see that Anderson is all right and Nora and when that is done I want to go to you and Daddy. For I am certain that there is a place where you wait for me, a place far beyond my flawed and frail perception. And so there is no goodbye for us. Things will happen as they are meant to happen. With the same logic that took you from me.

Thursday — 8:55 *a.m.*
Carter — hi —
It's your sweet ma
I love you, Carter
Please don't leave me

Later — Carter — Father Flynn said yesterday — something intervened — an accident, an avalanche. I am at the end of my life. When all has been put right for Anderson, I can be with you and Daddy — not until then. Wait for me. Wait to welcome me.

Wednesday — Carter — I've lost all sense of time since it happened. I read your poem a while ago —

today. "Sonnenkinder." Did you already know what was ahead? Carter, I feel the logic in what happened is something you know now. Something Daddy knows too now. Something I will not know until I am with you.

Thursday — Carter — another day has gone by. I miss you. Sometimes I feel you are close by. Then there are times you are lost to me, but inside the pain is there and I know it will never go away. Carter, I didn't understand what happened to me as a child and I don't understand what's happening now. I don't understand anything anymore. All I understand is pain.

Saturday — Carter, I believe beyond what has happened that there is a force, a Great Intelligence that is God — that nothing could have stopped you leaving as you did. That you know why now, that you are with Daddy — that you both know why, and someday Andy and I will know and understand the logic of what happened.

Thursday — Carter — I have my own agenda, as my friend Virginia used to say. Not now. Not yet. But soon. Soon as I put it right for Anderson.

Tuesday — Carter — I talked to Oliver's mother. She said you came to her, that you were in a fetal position. Then you got up and talked to her and were happy. And she asked you to stay. But you said no, you had to go. Carter, come to me. Don't leave me. Carter, I didn't know you were so fragile. I thought you were like me. There's a place deep inside me that is hard as a diamond and as bright, a place that came to be after what happened to me as a child. But maybe I was *born* with it, maybe it was always there, from the beginning. I thought it was there in you too, because you are my son. Carter, don't leave me. I was the first face you saw and the last, but I couldn't give you my strength to save you. There is a reason, a logic, in what has happened that I do not understand yet, a logic and a reason for all accidents that intervene.

(No date) — It doesn't matter. Carter, I'm below sea level. Still I breathe. Still I talk. Still I move. My brain goes back and forth to different levels. I never take off the locket Pearson gave me which has inside it pictures of you, Pearson, Linny, and me taken the day we were all together at Princeton for your graduation. The one of you has stuck to the glass inside the locket. I'll never be able to pull it loose for fear it will tear. I kept puzzling over how it got wet, why it sticks

to the glass, and then I realized it's from tears pouring out, down onto my face, on down like a stream to the sea. To you — Carter — don't leave me. G. asked me if I "looked over" — no, I didn't do that. I ran downstairs and I was going to go down to you on the street but instead I went in to where Nora was in the kitchen to tell her. It was fatal. I knew that right away. You had already left.

Sunday — I reside deeper below sea level. Yesterday, walking Eighty-eighth — West Side — tree-lined street, dappled sun, past an open third-floor window — piano — someone playing — I heard it as I walked by — a gate in front of the house was open, only a little, the door to the house closed. I stood there for a long time looking at it — wanting to walk through the gate, open the door, go up the stairs to the room on the third floor where the piano was playing — I wanted to *become* someone else — someone out of pain — close, so close to whoever is in that room playing the piano.

Is it you, Carter, in that room playing the piano? You'll stop playing as you hear me opening the door, running up the stairs to you, you'll know who it is. . . .

(No date) — I go over it, again and again, over it — What's going on, what's going on? Nothing's going on.

I'm here and Nora's here and everybody's here. . . .
But you didn't hear me. You moved fast out into the
hall. I followed you fast — Carter, come in and let's
talk! I was almost screaming, panicked . . . and I
reached out to pull you into the library but you ran
fast fast up the stairs and I ran after you fast fast calling out — Carter, come here, I have to talk to you!
You were running fast and strong up the stairs, so fast
I couldn't catch you. The room was empty and I ran
to the terrace and you were sitting on the wall far
from me, about twelve feet away, on my right side
with your right foot on the wall and your left foot on
the ground. Carter, what are you doing there? I
screamed at you — I went towards you but you put
your right hand up like a cop — straight out, palm
up — No, no, no, you said, don't come near. Don't
do this to me, I screamed, don't do this to Anderson,
don't do this to Daddy — my arm was straight out
reaching towards you as I screamed. Will I ever feel
again? you said. I screamed, Yes, you will, I know
what pain is and I can help you, Dr. Young can help
you, and I started down on my knees with both
arms stretched out, calling to you — Carter, I beg
you, and I was going to say, I'm your mother, but I
didn't, because you shouted No no no to me, don't do
that — and I got off my knees and stood there reaching out to you. Do you want me to get Dr. Young on

the phone? I screamed. Do you know his number? you said. No, I said, and you stood up and called out clearly the number — then you screamed out Fuck you and I started towards you but you sat back on the wall and put your hand up like a cop and said No no no and I screamed at you, Carter, come back come back, and you came back. I kept screaming to you — then a helicopter came overhead and you looked up at it, then at me, and reached out your hand to me and I went towards you and you put your hand up again against me and I stopped going towards you — then like a gymnast you deftly went in one motion over the wall and held on to it, hanging down over the river edge — so that for a moment I thought you were going to come back again, the way a gymnast would swing back onto a pole or bar he had been sitting on — then you didn't lose your grip, you didn't fall, you just let go.

Monday — Carter — to go into that room where the piano is playing, to become someone else, someone who is out of pain, finding you there, as I told Anderson I would, you'd stop playing the piano as I ran up the stairs, opening the door, saying to me, Hi, sweet Ma, as we hugged each other, then I'd look into your eyes, close, so close we would be.

⌒

Tuesday — Carter — when you came into my dressing room after it had been redone and saw the sofa and two chairs in front of the fireplace — Oh, Mom, you said, it's such a hopeful room. I wanted to say to you, It's a room we'll talk in and have happy times in together — but I was afraid. Afraid I'd make you pull away from me. Oh God, help me.

Wednesday — Carter — when it happened it was like being on a roller coaster, nothing could have stopped it.

Saturday — Carter — I don't have to pretend anymore about anything. Carter — I know you loved me and you knew I loved you. Destiny.

Sunday — Carter — Hattie came to see me today. She's started at Yale Law School. She's living in the Taft Apartments, where Andy lived last year. He came home too — the weekend. He's exhausted and so am I. This morning I could hardly move. I lay on the bed most of the day and cried. Sometimes I think we're all in a dream — Andy, Pearson, Hattie here today, Matt and Ruth coming so often to be with me — I'm going to wake up and call you and tell you: Carter, I had the most terrible dream, and then I'll recount it all to you and halfway through you'll say —

Oh, sweet Ma, it's only a dream, everything's all right.
I pray to God to help me.

Friday — Carter — sometimes you are here so close — today, not present in that way. Are you all right? Are you with Daddy? Are you close to me as you are close together? Is it going to be all right — or am I going through the door to you?

58

As strangers we entered the room of the support group I joined, but later, sitting in a circle, we were not strangers, not even friends, we were a family, one that does not judge, for pain had stripped us bare. Ah yes . . . we knew each other well.

After our meetings I would walk home and find myself in a park stopping beneath a tree to circle the trunk with my arms, to feel my spirit merge on up to the branches, on up to the sky above. I felt wordless communication with strangers passing. Others sitting at outdoor cafés, a woman walking her dog, were not alien to me, nor was I to them, I knew their pain, their joy — yes, even joy — for although I resided in a dimension where even the memory of it seemed forever lost to me, I knew joy existed somewhere for others. I too had once had it in my life. No one would ever be a stranger to me again, for I knew that if it had not come already, the day *would* come when they would have to live through tragedy and loss as we all do and this connected us, not only now but forever. By giving myself to the visceral pain that possessed and consumed me, by not fighting it, as each moment passed I gained strength, more than I'd had the moment before, and with this came an overpowering will to survive, because if I could it might help others who had experienced tragedy, for anyone who meets such testings of the soul without escaping into a glass bubble is helping to quicken the vibrations of the whole earth.

59

Carter — it was terrible coming here without you. The A's left the rooms disordered, furniture out of place, mantels in disarray. I couldn't move, and cried and cried. Andy started putting things back in place, furniture, objects, trying to calm me. I don't know what's going to happen. If Andy were not here I would be with you and Daddy. Daddy loved me but I was flawed, flawed from the time I was nine. Before that it was all right. But none of that matters now. I have to breathe in and out to stay alive.

Friday — Carter, I feel there is something I could have done to stop it from happening. I torment myself that we were in some terrible collaboration together. That maybe I should follow you into that dark land. But already I am there, on one plateau or another, there is no surcease. Will it be forever so? Help me, help me to understand. I must remain here for Anderson, but soon I will put things right for him and then I can go, can't I?

Monday — Carter — a dream hallucination of you and our darling Nenna far away, walking away from me side by side on the beach — you in your black coat, Nenna in black, her hair hanging down her back — side by side you walked away, together, but not touching each other.

Sunday — Carter — sometimes I feel you close by, then a long time and you are not. I am beginning to believe that death, as we know it here, is only a leaving of one dimension for another that is also on this planet, and that those who have left have broken the barrier and are there, and although we cannot see them they surround us. Yes, I am more certain now than ever that death is simply a change of the dimension we are now in to another, close to us, although we cannot break through to it yet — but we will, for everything happens at the right moment, the acceptable *time* — and that this life is something we dream through, consisting of beauty and nightmares, and someday it will all come together and we will be free to join each other. Stay close to me. I need to feel you close by.

Wednesday — Carter — Please don't leave me. I haven't felt you near in quite a while.

Sunday (Juniper Room, Galisteo Inn, Galisteo, New Mexico) — Carter — there is great peace, great quiet here. At my first session at the Light Institute with a facilitator, Karen, I talked about you, about how it happened, how I don't understand but believe that it's part of the plan, the design — nothing could have been done to prevent it. We talked for about an hour. Then I undressed and lay on a high bed with my knees over a pillow, blankets over me. The room is small, white, silent — all is calm. The rug on the floor is aqua. Above the bed is a window to the sky. Heavy wood beams support the ceiling. I lay with eyes open for a time. Karen, standing behind my head, held it in her hands and after a time touched my neck and ears as I breathed deeply. My eyes closed and I entered a hypnotic state. This session was to concentrate on the emotional center and the higher center.

I envisioned a white light going through the top of my head, going on down into my chest, the touch of her hands sending it into my stomach, which became sore, and I could feel a hard ball of glutinous texture there. I envisioned it as an embryo, an embryo who was me, who felt unworthy to be born, who wanted more than anything else to be loved, who was *afraid*. Then the embryo became warm and decided to be born. It rose up to Karen's hands. A golden light suffused me as it moved up into my head — higher — and I imagined becoming an ancient tree rooted in earth with tall branches reaching to the sky like the tree outside the window at the inn. But these branches had leaves and flowers and a nest in the tree and within it an egg that held a bird that broke free and flew away, and as it did, the tree cracked asunder and I was free.

The embryo gave me a gift of golden light so that I would not be afraid.

Carter, are you close by? Are we separated only by a veil?

Later — Being here — the desert — the silence. I feel something is going to happen, then I know that it *has* happened — what is going to happen already has.

Thursday — Carter — I love you, I miss you, I feel so alone. I'm doing the best I can but I want to be with you and Daddy. I'm in some deep place where no one can reach me. Andy's doing O.K., I think. I really do. So why not go? Perhaps I will if I could only go in a way that would not hurt him. L. always said "pray to Divine Mother" and I was never able to but I can now. I understand in a way I didn't before. I admire Andy more than I can say for his courage. If only Daddy were here now to help me. Sometimes I feel so close to him and also to you. I never felt I could please Daddy, but then I did so much that was wrong. The happiest moments with you were in SH that summer I had my show at Cord Gallery — Anderson hadn't been born yet — you and Daddy and me driving around in the car at night — remember — I'd sing to you, holding you and rocking you to sleep — ". . . he's a noodle, he's a google" — making up silly words to the tune of "On the Back Porch." Oh God, oh God, oh God. A few days ago I was thinking of that summer — of supreme happiness. Those times which come to us are the truth of ourselves, the truth of our lives, and even though we have few — it is enough. It will suffice to not have lived in vain.

After giving birth.

Daybreak — infant Carter stirs, smiles, hands reach up, face comes towards me — his spirit emerging from chrysalis or egg. . . .

The moment on the terrace with S.L. — he

touched my hair — close, so close, and we saw each other plain — but it was I who pulled away. . . .

Day after day for a whole week that summer in Southampton I've just told you about.

Standing on the stairs before the party, our house-warming — Daddy looked at me — the joy he took in me — love surrounding me with no word said.

After late, late rehearsal the night before opening in the play, S.L. and I falling asleep exhausted. Dawn, and "I awake to find you — gone." I cried out — then suddenly he was beside me, holding me, saying — upset by the rendering of the leaves on trees of the set, couldn't sleep, gone back to the theater, on a ladder until now, painting, trying to improve the rendering so that when I appeared on stage I would be presented handsomely.

Moments — many — when I'm painting.

In the chartered plane with L.S. when it crashed. Our other passenger hysterical. As we tumbled out onto the prairie, wild fields, nothing except mountains, around us — L., as if nothing had happened, serenely leaning over and picking a flower at his feet, saying to the shaken pilot, "Ah — what is the name of this flower, do you know?"

The summer after Daddy died, Carter and Polly bicycling along the dunes. Her corn-silk hair tousled, flirty, laughing, washed in sunlight. I was on the porch when they returned — a party was going on in the garden next door — and we went into the house, up the curved staircase leading to the balcony of the tower — to sit on the banquette by the window — giggling, enchanted, unperceived by the guests below as we commented on them milling around our neighbor's pool, chitty-chattering away, posing with their cool drinks, the women in pretty summer dresses, the men in blazers. Then Carter leaned over to touch a sprig of grass tangled in Polly's hair — as he did, the light changed, filtered through the shutters, and as he reached towards her, I became the sun covering them with light — Polly, beautiful Polly, his first love. . . .

Summertime — Daddy and I on the porch, together on the swing at the end of the day, quietly talking. . . .

Early dinner — that strange light, was it dusk or dawn? Daddy and I, as we sat in the dining room, a silence, and then the sound of a mourning dove . . . we look at each other and I see in his eyes our beginning and our end, I see it there because he has seen it in mine.

Greenwich — the week in August before Stan was born, walking in the fields with L., gathering Queen Anne's lace.

From across the road Al's mother calling — Al-les-san-dro — that summer — that golden summer.

The moment painting the carousel horse on the porch — I looked up at Daddy and he said, "You're happy, aren't you?" And I was, yes, completely.

Yes, *happiness* — they are moments enough to have made my life not in vain. That I had meant something to Daddy who loved me. To others who have loved me although I was and am *flawed*. Oh Divine Mother, help me to help myself. It's so strange, S.L. living down the block. Am I ever in his mind, I wonder — or not at all? Oh S., my mouse. We'll all be together someday — in light — in peace. I have to believe that. Pray to Divine Mother. Carter, help me. Daddy, help me.

The blue light still comes to me. You are with me.

60

A SUICIDE is defined by the *Random House Dictionary* as "a person who intentionally takes his or her own life." Often, later, when Carter's friends from Princeton and I talked, they said that whenever discussions came up about suicide, Carter had always said it was something that he himself could never do. What happened was an aberration, like a stroke, or lightning hitting unexpectedly. It may have been triggered by his allergy doctor's prescription.

But I still don't know, none of us do, the *reason* why it happened or what demons took possession of his fantasies as he slept so deeply on the sofa in the library that staggeringly hot July day — I believe someday we will, and it will fit into place like the last piece of a puzzle, and when it does we will understand that there *is* a reason why terrible things happen in the world — we will understand the tragedies that come to us — understand *why,* in the same way that we now understand joy but do not question it. The day will come — maybe sooner than we think — when it will be made clear and, simplistic though it sounds, I believe the answer itself will be so simple, so right, so true, that when we do understand, we shall no longer cry out *Why, God, why?*— for with understanding we shall be out of pain, out of darkness into light. It takes a great leap of faith to believe this, but I do, and in some measure it has brought me peace.

61

EACH DAY, each year that passes as I live with Carter's death, I come to see it in perspective of the tragedies that have happened and are happening every day in our world — the Holocaust, Rwanda, Bosnia — tragedies so indescribable that one mother's pain is maybe not so important after all. Except to me, of course. But perhaps in some small way it will be to you — perhaps if you are suffering from loss and feel you can't go on, it will reach you, for what I am trying to say to you is: Don't give up, don't ever give up, because without pain there cannot be joy, and both are what make us know we are alive. You have the courage to let the pain you feel possess you, the courage not to deny it, and if you do this the day will come when you wake and know that you are working through it, and because you are, there is a hope, small though it may be, a hope you can trust, and the more you allow yourself to trust it, the more it will tell you that although nothing will ever be the same, and the suffering you are working through will be with you always — you *will* come through, and when you do you'll know who you really are, and someday there will be moments when you will be able to love again, and laugh again, and live again. I hope this will come true for you as it has for me.

THERE IS a Queen Anne chest with smoky mirrored doors in my room. The room it's in now is different from the one it was in when Carter was in his first year, the place different too. He used to have difficulty falling asleep at night, and Daddy and I would take turns holding him over our shoulder, dancing to the Jobim bossa nova music he loved. As they twirled around the room their reflections would now and then drift past — Carter's head resting on Daddy's shoulder, snug in the blanket he was held in. Now when I look in the mirrored doors, Carter and Daddy are not there, even the echo of their shadows has gone. They exist only in my mind's eye — clear to me as they were then. The small wisteria plant Daddy planted outside the house we lived in then is still there although we are not, and the wisteria can be seen — only it has grown and multiplied, spreading almost over the graystone house, reaching far up to the fifth story and on over the roof. I connect these two things because they are rooted together in my memory — of a place, a time of happiness, so secure it never occurred to me that it wouldn't last forever.

A NOTE ON THE TYPE

This book was set in Fairfield, the first typeface from the hand of the distinguished American artist and engraver Rudolph Ruzicka (1883–1978). In its structure Fairfield displays the sober and sane qualities of the master craftsman whose talent has long been dedicated to clarity. It is this trait that accounts for the trim grace and vigor, the spirited design and sensitive balance, of this original typeface. Rudolph Ruzicka was born in Bohemia and came to America in 1894. He designed and illustrated many books, and was the creator of a considerable list of individual prints — wood engravings, line engravings on copper, and aquatints.

Composed by NK Graphics,
Keene, New Hampshire
Printed and bound by R. R. Donnelley & Sons,
Harrisonburg, Virginia
Designed by Misha Beletsky